HYPOTHYROIDISM COOKBOOK

MAIN COURSE - 60+ Easy to prepare home recipes for a balanced and healthy diet

TABLE OF CONTENTS

BREAKFAST...6

BLUEBERRY PANCAKES...6

MULBERRIES PANCAKES..7

BANANA PANCAKES..8

NECTARINE PANCAKES...9

PANCAKES...10

PEACHES MUFFINS..11

LEMON MUFFINS..12

BLUEBERRY MUFFINS..13

KUMQUAT MUFFINS..14

CHOCOLATE MUFFINS..15

MUFFINS..16

OMELETTE...17

CARROT OMELETTE..18

ONION OMELETTE...19

BROCCOLI OMELETTE..20

BEETS OMELETTE...21

EGGPLANT ROLLATINI...22

ASPARAGUS WITH EGG...23

DEVILED EGGS...24

SPICY CUCUMBERS..25

LUNCH..26

HUMMUS PITA..26

BUTTERNUT SQUASH...27

BROCCOLI SOUP..29

CHICKEN NOODLE SOUP 31

TORTILLA SOUP 33

ASPARAGUS SOUP 34

LENTIL SOUP 35

BURRITO BOWL 37

TURKEY BURGER AND SPINACH 38

EASY PIZZA 39

CRANBERRY SALAD 40

ITALIAN SALAD 41

CHICKPEA COLESLAW 42

ROMAINE SALAD 43

GRAIN SALAD 44

QUINOA SALAD 45

WEDGE SALAD...46

COUSCOUS SALAD..47

FARRO SALAD 48

THAI MANGO SALAD 49

DINNER 50

SIMPLE PIZZA RECIPE 50

ZUCCHINI PIZZA..51

CAULIFLOWER RECIPE 52

BROCCOLI RECIPE 53

TOMATOES & HAM PIZZA 54

LEEK SOUP 55

ZUCCHINI SOUP..56

RUTABAGA SOUP 57

CARROT SOUP 58

YAMS SOUP 59

SMOOTHIES 60

PEANUT BUTTER SMOOTHIE...60

PINEAPPLE SMOOTHIE 61

5 INGREDIENTS SMOOTHIE..62

STRAWBERRY SMOOTHIE...63

MANGO SMOOTHIE 64

SPINACH SMOOTHIE 65

OATS SMOOTHIE..66

BERRY BEAN SMOOTHIE...67

ORANGE SMOOTHIE...68

BLUEBERRIES SMOOTHIE 69

accounting, officially permitted, or otherwise, qualified services. If advice is necessary, legal or professional, a practiced individual in the profession should be ordered.

- From a Declaration of Principles which was accepted and approved equally by a Committee of the American Bar Association and a Committee of Publishers and Associations.

Introduction

Hypothyroidism recipes for personal enjoyment but also for family enjoyment. You will love them for sure for how easy it is to prepare them.

BREAKFAST

BLUEBERRY PANCAKES

Serves: **4**

Prep Time: **10** Minutes

Cook Time: **20** Minutes

Total Time: **30** Minutes

INGREDIENTS

- 1 cup whole wheat flour
- ¼ tsp baking soda
- ¼ tsp baking powder
- 1 cup blueberries
- 2 eggs
- 1 cup milk

DIRECTIONS

1. In a bowl combine all ingredients together and mix well
2. In a skillet heat olive oil
3. Pour ¼ of the batter and cook each pancake for 1-2 minutes per side
4. When ready remove from heat and serve

MULBERRIES PANCAKES

Serves: **4**
Prep Time: **10** Minutes

Cook Time: **30** Minutes

Total Time: **40** Minutes

INGREDIENTS

- 1 cup whole wheat flour
- ¼ tsp baking soda
- ¼ tsp baking powder
- 1 cup mulberries
- 2 eggs
- 1 cup milk

DIRECTIONS

1. In a bowl combine all ingredients together and mix well
2. In a skillet heat olive oil
3. Pour ¼ of the batter and cook each pancake for 1-2 minutes per side
4. When ready remove from heat and serve

Serves: *4*

Prep Time: *10*   Minutes

Cook Time: *20*   Minutes

Total Time: *30*   Minutes

INGREDIENTS

- 1 cup whole wheat flour
- ¼ tsp baking soda
- ¼ tsp baking powder
- 1 cup mashed banana
- 2 eggs
- 1 cup milk

DIRECTIONS

1. In a bowl combine all ingredients together and mix well
2. In a skillet heat olive oil
3. Pour ¼ of the batter and cook each pancake for 1-2 minutes per side
4. When ready remove from heat and serve

NECTARINE PANCAKES

Serves: **4**

Prep Time: **10**   Minutes

Cook Time: **20**   Minutes

Total Time: **30**   Minutes

INGREDIENTS

- 1 cup whole wheat flour
- ¼ tsp baking soda
- ¼ tsp baking powder
- 1 cup nectarines
- 2 eggs
- 1 cup milk

DIRECTIONS

1. In a bowl combine all ingredients together and mix well
2. In a skillet heat olive oil
3. Pour ¼ of the batter and cook each pancake for 1-2 minutes per side
4. When ready remove from heat and serve

PANCAKES

Serves: *4*

Prep Time: *10*   Minutes

Cook Time: *30*   Minutes

Total Time: *40*   Minutes

INGREDIENTS

- 1 cup whole wheat flour
- ¼ tsp baking soda
- ¼ tsp baking powder
- 2 eggs
- 1 cup milk

DIRECTIONS

1. In a bowl combine all ingredients together and mix well
2. In a skillet heat olive oil
3. Pour ¼ of the batter and cook each pancake for 1-2 minutes per side
4. When ready remove from heat and serve

PEACHES MUFFINS

Serves: **8-12**

Prep Time: **10**   Minutes

Cook Time: **20**   Minutes

Total Time: **30**   Minutes

INGREDIENTS

- 2 eggs
- 1 tablespoon olive oil
- 1 cup milk
- 2 cups whole wheat flour
- 1 tsp baking soda
- ¼ tsp baking soda
- 1 cup peaches
- 1 tsp cinnamon
- ¼ cup molasses

DIRECTIONS

1. In a bowl combine all wet ingredients
2. In another bowl combine all dry ingredients
3. Combine wet and dry ingredients together
4. Pour mixture into 8-12 prepared muffin cups, fill 2/3 of the cups
5. Bake for 18-20 minutes at 375 F, when ready remove and serve

LEMON MUFFINS

Serves: *8-12*

Prep Time: *10*   Minutes

Cook Time: *20*   Minutes

Total Time: *30*   Minutes

INGREDIENTS

- 2 eggs
- 1 tablespoon olive oil
- 1 cup milk
- 2 cups whole wheat flour
- 1 tsp baking soda
- ¼ tsp baking soda
- 1 tsp cinnamon
- 1 cup lemon slices

DIRECTIONS

1. In a bowl combine all wet ingredients
2. In another bowl combine all dry ingredients
3. Combine wet and dry ingredients together
4. Pour mixture into 8-12 prepared muffin cups, fill 2/3 of the cups
5. Bake for 18-20 minutes at 375 F
6. When ready remove from the oven and serve

BLUEBERRY MUFFINS

Serves: **8-12**

Prep Time: **10** Minutes

Cook Time: **20** Minutes

Total Time: **30** Minutes

INGREDIENTS

- 2 eggs
- 1 tablespoon olive oil
- 1 cup milk
- 2 cups whole wheat flour
- 1 tsp baking soda
- ¼ tsp baking soda
- 1 tsp cinnamon
- 1 cup blueberries

DIRECTIONS

1. In a bowl combine all wet ingredients
2. In another bowl combine all dry ingredients
3. Combine wet and dry ingredients together
4. Fold in blueberries and mix well
5. Pour mixture into 8-12 prepared muffin cups, fill 2/3 of the cups
6. Bake for 18-20 minutes at 375 F, when ready remove and serve

KUMQUAT MUFFINS

Serves: *8-12*

Prep Time: *10*   Minutes

Cook Time: *20*   Minutes

Total Time: *30*   Minutes

INGREDIENTS

- 2 eggs
- 1 tablespoon olive oil
- 1 cup milk
- 2 cups whole wheat flour
- 1 tsp baking soda
- ¼ tsp baking soda
- 1 tsp cinnamon
- 1 cup kumquat

DIRECTIONS

1. In a bowl combine all wet ingredients
2. In another bowl combine all dry ingredients
3. Combine wet and dry ingredients together
4. Pour mixture into 8-12 prepared muffin cups, fill 2/3 of the cups
5. Bake for 18-20 minutes at 375 F
6. When ready remove from the oven and serve

CHOCOLATE MUFFINS

Serves: **8-12**

Prep Time: **10**   Minutes

Cook Time: **20**   Minutes

Total Time: **30**   Minutes

INGREDIENTS

- 2 eggs
- 1 tablespoon olive oil
- 1 cup milk
- 2 cups whole wheat flour
- 1 tsp baking soda
- ¼ tsp baking soda
- 1 tsp cinnamon
- 1 cup chocolate chips

DIRECTIONS

1. In a bowl combine all dry ingredients
2. In another bowl combine all dry ingredients
3. Combine wet and dry ingredients together
4. Fold in chocolate chips and mix well
5. Pour mixture into 8-12 prepared muffin cups, fill 2/3 of the cups
6. Bake for 18-20 minutes at 375 F, when ready remove and serve

Serves: **8-12**

Prep Time: **10**   Minutes

Cook Time: **20**   Minutes

Total Time: **30**   Minutes

INGREDIENTS

- 2 eggs
- 1 tablespoon olive oil
- 1 cup milk
- 2 cups whole wheat flour
- 1 tsp baking soda
- ¼ tsp baking soda
- 1 tsp cinnamon

DIRECTIONS

1. In a bowl combine all wet ingredients
2. In another bowl combine all dry ingredients
3. Combine wet and dry ingredients together
4. Pour mixture into 8-12 prepared muffin cups, fill 2/3 of the cups
5. Bake for 18-20 minutes at 375 F
6. When ready remove from the oven and serve

OMELETTE

Serves: *1*
Prep Time: *5*   Minutes
Cook Time: *10*   Minutes
Total Time: *15*   Minutes

INGREDIENTS

- 2 eggs
- ¼ tsp salt
- ¼ tsp black pepper
- 1 tablespoon olive oil
- ¼ cup cheese
- ¼ tsp basil

DIRECTIONS

1. In a bowl combine all ingredients together and mix well
2. In a skillet heat olive oil and pour the egg mixture
3. Cook for 1-2 minutes per side
4. When ready remove omelette from the skillet and serve

CARROT OMELETTE

Serves: **1**

Prep Time: **5** Minutes

Cook Time: **10** Minutes

Total Time: **15** Minutes

INGREDIENTS

- 2 eggs
- ¼ tsp salt
- ¼ tsp black pepper
- 1 tablespoon olive oil
- ¼ cup cheese
- ¼ tsp basil
- 1 cup carrot

DIRECTIONS

1. In a bowl combine all ingredients together and mix well
2. In a skillet heat olive oil and pour the egg mixture
3. Cook for 1-2 minutes per side
4. When ready remove omelette from the skillet and serve

ONION OMELETTE

Serves: *1*
Prep Time: *5*   Minutes

Cook Time: *10*   Minutes

Total Time: *15*   Minutes

INGREDIENTS

- 2 eggs
- ¼ tsp salt
- ¼ tsp black pepper
- 1 tablespoon olive oil
- ¼ cup cheese
- ¼ tsp basil
- 1 cup red onion

DIRECTIONS

1. In a bowl combine all ingredients together and mix well
2. In a skillet heat olive oil and pour the egg mixture
3. Cook for 1-2 minutes per side
4. When ready remove omelette from the skillet and serve

BROCCOLI OMELETTE

Serves: **1**

Prep Time: **5**   Minutes

Cook Time: **10**   Minutes

Total Time: **15**   Minutes

INGREDIENTS

- 2 eggs
- ¼ tsp salt
- ¼ tsp black pepper
- 1 tablespoon olive oil
- ¼ cup cheese
- ¼ tsp basil
- 1 cup broccoli

DIRECTIONS

1. In a bowl combine all ingredients together and mix well
2. In a skillet heat olive oil and pour the egg mixture
3. Cook for 1-2 minutes per side
4. When ready remove omelette from the skillet and serve

BEETS OMELETTE

Serves: **1**

Prep Time: **5** Minutes

Cook Time: **10** Minutes

Total Time: **15** Minutes

INGREDIENTS

- 2 eggs
- ¼ tsp salt
- ¼ tsp black pepper
- 1 tablespoon olive oil
- ¼ cup cheese
- ¼ tsp basil
- 1 cup beets

DIRECTIONS

1. In a bowl combine all ingredients together and mix well
2. In a skillet heat olive oil and pour the egg mixture
3. Cook for 1-2 minutes per side
4. When ready remove omelette from the skillet and serve

Serves: **6-8**

Prep Time: **10**   Minutes

Cook Time: **25**   Minutes

Total Time: **35**   Minutes

INGREDIENTS

- 1 eggplant
- 12 oz. ricotta cheese
- 2 oz. mozzarella cheese
- 1 can tomatoes
- ¼ tsp salt
- 2 tablespoons seasoning

DIRECTIONS

1. Lay the eggplant on a baking sheet
2. Roast at 350 F for 12-15 minutes
3. In a bowl combine mozzarella, seasoning, tomatoes, ricotta cheese and salt
4. Add cheese mixture to the eggplant and roll
5. Place the rolls into a baking dish and bake for another 10-12 minutes
6. When ready remove from the oven and serve

Serves: **4-6**
Prep Time: **10** Minutes

Cook Time: **25** Minutes

Total Time: **35** Minutes

INGREDIENTS

- 1 lb. asparagus
- 4-5 pieces prosciutto
- ¼ tsp salt
- 2 eggs

DIRECTIONS

1. Trim the asparagus and season with salt
2. Wrap each asparagus pieces with prosciutto
3. Place the wrapped asparagus in a baking dish
4. Bake at 375 F for 22-25 minutes
5. When ready remove from the oven and serve

DEVILED EGGS

Serves: *8*

Prep Time: *10*   Minutes

Cook Time: *20*   Minutes

Total Time: *30*   Minutes

INGREDIENTS

- 8 eggs
- ½ cup Greek Yogurt
- 1 tablespoon mustard
- 1 tsp smoked paprika
- 1 tablespoon green onions

DIRECTIONS

1. In a saucepan add the eggs and bring to a boil
2. Cover and boil for 10-15 minutes
3. When ready slice the eggs in half and remove the yolks
4. In a bowl combine remaining ingredients and mix well
5. Spoon 1 tablespoon of the mixture into each egg
6. Garnish with green onions and serve

SPICY CUCUMBERS

Serves: **6-8**

Prep Time: **5**   Minutes

Cook Time: **15**   Minutes

Total Time: **20**   Minutes

INGREDIENTS

- 2 cucumbers
- 1 cup Greek yogurt
- 1 garlic clove
- 1 tsp paprika
- 1 tsp dill
- 1 tsp chili powder

DIRECTIONS

1. In a bowl combine all ingredients together except cucumbers
2. Cut the cucumbers into rounds and scoot out the inside
3. Fill each cucumber with the spicy mixture
4. When ready sprinkle paprika and serve

LUNCH

HUMMUS PITA

Serves: **1**

Prep Time: **5**   Minutes

Cook Time: **10**   Minutes

Total Time: **15**   Minutes

INGREDIENTS

- ½ cup spinach
- 1 ½ tbs pine nuts
- ¼ cup hummus
- 2 eggs
- ¼ cup tomato
- 1 pita

DIRECTIONS

1. Boil the eggs until hard
2. Cut the pita in half
3. Fill both halves with the remaining ingredients
4. Serve immediately

BUTTERNUT SQUASH

Serves: **6**

Prep Time: **10**   Minutes

Cook Time: **60**   Minutes

Total Time: **70**   Minutes

INGREDIENTS

- 1 tsp thyme
- 15 oz chicken broth
- ½ cup apple juice
- 1 ½ tbs olive oil
- 1 celery stalk
- 1 cup parmesan
- 2 leeks
- 2 carrots
- 2 lb butternut squash
- Salt
- Pepper

DIRECTIONS

1. Cut the squash and drizzle with oil, then season with salt and pepper
2. Bake in the preheated oven at 350 F for at least 50 minutes

3. Cook the leeks, carrots and celery for 15 minutes in hot oil until softened

4. Scrape squash into processor and discard peel

5. Pour in 1 cup of broth and puree until smooth

6. Mix in apple juice and season with salt and pepper

7. Garnish each bowl with parmesan cheese and serve

BROCCOLI SOUP

Serves: **2**

Prep Time: **10**   Minutes

Cook Time: **10**   Minutes

Total Time: **20**   Minutes

INGREDIENTS

- 1 onion
- 2 cloves garlic
- 1 tbs butter
- 2 cup broccoli
- 1 potato
- 3 cup chicken broth
- 1 cup cheddar cheese
- 1/3 cup buttermilk
- Salt
- Pepper

DIRECTIONS

1. Cook the onion and garlic in melted butter for 5 minutes
2. Add the diced potato, broccoli florets and chicken broth
3. Bring to a boil, then reduce the heat and simmer for at least 5 minutes
4. Allow to cool, then pulse until smooth using a blender

5. Return to the saucepan and add the buttermilk and ¼ cup cheese
6. Cook for about 3 minutes
7. Season with salt and pepper
8. Serve topped with the remaining cheese

Serves: **6**

Prep Time: **40** Minutes

Cook Time: **80** Minutes

Total Time: **120** Minutes

INGREDIENTS

Broth:
- 15 peppercorns
- 2 onions
- 2 carrots
- 1 rib celery
- 3 sprigs thyme
- 5 cloves garlic
- 3 bay leaves
- 8 chicken thighs

Soup:
- 2 chicken bouillon cubes
- 1 tsp salt
- 5 oz egg noodles
- 1/3 cup parsley
- 2 ribs celery
- 2 carrots

DIRECTIONS

1. Place the broth ingredients in a pot with 12 cups of water
2. Bring to a boil, then reduce the heat and simmer for about 20 minutes
3. Remove the chicken and shred meat from bones
4. Return the bones to the pot and continue to simmer for another 60 minutes
5. Strain the broth and discard the bones and other solids
6. Skim broth and bring to a boil
7. Add the soup ingredients except for the parsley
8. Stir in the noodles and cook for at least 5 minutes
9. Stir in the chicken meat and parsley and cook 1 more minute
10. Serve immediately

TORTILLA SOUP

Serves: **6**

Prep Time: **10**   Minutes

Cook Time: **10**   Minutes

Total Time: **20**   Minutes

INGREDIENTS

- 1/3 cup rice
- 15 oz salsa
- 1 can black beans
- 30 oz chicken broth
- 1 cup corn
- Chicken

DIRECTIONS

1. Place the broth and the salsa in a pot and bring to a boil
2. Add rice, beans and cooked chicken
3. Simmer covered for about 10 minutes
4. Stir in the corn
5. Serve topped with cheese

ASPARAGUS SOUP

Serves: **4**

Prep Time: **15** Minutes

Cook Time: **35** Minutes

Total Time: **50** Minutes

INGREDIENTS

- 2 tbs oil
- 1/3 tsp salt
- 1 cup bread cubes
- 1 cup potato
- 2 tsp horseradish
- 3 cups chicken broth
- 1 lb asparagus
- Scallions
- 1 shallot

DIRECTIONS

1. Cook the shallot until soft for 2 minutes
2. Add the asparagus, potato, broth, horseradish and salt and bring to a boil
3. Reduce the heat and simmer for about 15 minutes
4. Pulse using a blender
5. Cook the bread cubes in hot oil until crispy, serve with croutons

LENTIL SOUP

Serves: *9*
Prep Time: *10* Minutes

Cook Time: *50* Minutes

Total Time: *60* Minutes

INGREDIENTS

- 2 tbs oil
- 1 stalk celery
- 1 red bell pepper
- 2 cans chicken broth
- 1 onion
- 1 cup carrots
- 2 garlic cloves
- 2 tsp cumin
- 1 tsp coriander
- 1 can tomatoes
- 2 sweet potatoes
- 3 tsp thyme leaves
- 2 cups red lentils

DIRECTIONS

1. Cook the onion, celery, carrots and red pepper in hot oil for 3 minutes

2. Add garlic, thyme, cumin and coriander and cook for 10 more minutes

3. Add the broth, sweet potatoes, lentils and tomatoes

4. Bring to a boil, then reduce the heat and simmer for at least 30 minutes

5. Pulse using a blender

6. Serve immediately

Serves: *1*
Prep Time: *5*   Minutes

Cook Time: *5*   Minutes

Total Time: *10*   Minutes

INGREDIENTS

- 1 cup rice
- ½ cup roasted red peppers
- ½ cup black beans
- ½ cup shrimp
- 3 tbs salsa
- ½ avocado

DIRECTIONS

1. Cook the rice and the shrimp as you desire
2. Mix everything together
3. Serve topped with avocado slices

Serves: **1**

Prep Time: **10**   Minutes

Cook Time: **10**   Minutes

Total Time: **20**   Minutes

INGREDIENTS

- ½ cup ground turkey
- 1 hatch chile
- Salt
- Pepper
- 1 cup spinach
- 1 tomato
- 1 onion
- ½ avocado

DIRECTIONS

1. Mix the turkey meat with chiles, salt and pepper and form a patty
2. Grill until done
3. Serve on a bed of cooked spinach and top with tomatoes, onion and avocado slices
4. Serve immediately

Serves: **2**

Prep Time: **5**   Minutes

Cook Time: **10**   Minutes

Total Time: **15**   Minutes

INGREDIENTS

- ½ cup spinach
- 1 tbs basil
- 2 cloves garlic
- 1 onion
- ½ cup sun dried tomatoes
- 2 roasted peppers
- ½ cup chicken breast
- 1 wheat naan
- ½ cup mozzarella

DIRECTIONS

1. Top the naan with all of the ingredients
2. Bake for 10 minutes
3. Serve immediately

CRANBERRY SALAD

Serves: **2**

Prep Time: **5** Minutes

Cook Time: **5** Minutes

Total Time: **10** Minutes

INGREDIENTS

- 1 can unsweetened pineapple
- 1 package cherry gelatin
- 1 tablespoon lemon juice
- ½ cup artificial sweetener
- 1 cup cranberries
- 1 orange
- 1 cup celery
- ½ cup pecans

DIRECTIONS

1. In a bowl combine all ingredients together and mix well
2. Serve with dressing

Serves: **2**

Prep Time: **5**   Minutes

Cook Time: **5**   Minutes

Total Time: **10**   Minutes

INGREDIENTS

- 8 oz. romaine lettuce
- 2 cups radicchio
- ¼ red onion
- 2 ribs celery
- 1 cup tomatoes
- 1 can chickpeas
- 1 cup salad dressing

DIRECTIONS

1. In a bowl combine all ingredients together and mix well
2. Serve with dressing

Serves: **2**
Prep Time: **5**   Minutes

Cook Time: **5**   Minutes

Total Time: **10**   Minutes

INGREDIENTS

- 2 cans chickpeas
- 2 cups carrots
- 1 cup celery
- ¼ cup green onions
- ¼ cup dill leaves
- ¼ cup olive oil
- 1 cucumber
- 1 cup salad dressing

DIRECTIONS

1. In a bowl combine all ingredients together and mix well
2. Serve with dressing

Serves: **2**

Prep Time: **5**   Minutes

Cook Time: **5**   Minutes

Total Time: **10**   Minutes

INGREDIENTS

- 1 cup cooked quinoa
- 1 cup sunflower seeds
- 1 tablespoon olive oil
- 1 head romaine lettuce
- 1 cup carrots
- 1 cup cabbage
- ¼ cup radishes

DIRECTIONS

1. In a bowl combine all ingredients together and mix well
2. Serve with dressing

Serves: 2

Prep Time: 5   Minutes

Cook Time: 5   Minutes

Total Time: 10   Minutes

INGREDIENTS

- 1 bunch coriander leaves
- 1 bunch mint leaves
- ¼ red onion
- 1 bunch parsley
- 1 cup lentils
- 1 tablespoon pumpkin seeds
- 1 tablespoon pine nuts

DIRECTIONS

1. In a bowl combine all ingredients together and mix well
2. Serve with dressing

QUINOA SALAD

Serves: **2**

Prep Time: **5**   Minutes

Cook Time: **5**   Minutes

Total Time: **10** Minutes

INGREDIENTS

- 1 cauliflower
- 2 cups cooked quinoa
- 1 can chickpeas
- 1 cup baby spinach
- ¼ cup parsley
- ¼ cup cilantro
- ¼ cup green onion
- ½ cup feta cheese

DIRECTIONS

1. In a bowl combine all ingredients together and mix well
2. Serve with dressing

Serves: **2**

Prep Time: **5**   Minutes

Cook Time: **5**   Minutes

Total Time: **10** Minutes

INGREDIENTS

- 1 head romaine lettuce
- 1 cup tomatoes
- 1 cup cucumber
- 1 cup celery
- ¼ cup olives
- 1 shallot
- 1 cup salad dressing

DIRECTIONS

1. In a bowl combine all ingredients together and mix well
2. Serve with dressing

COUSCOUS SALAD

Serves: **2**

Prep Time: **5**   Minutes

Cook Time: **5**   Minutes

Total Time: **10**   Minutes

INGREDIENTS

- 1 cup couscous
- ¼ cup pine nuts
- ¼ cup olive lil
- 1 tablespoon lemon juice
- 1 shallot
- 2 cloves garlic
- 1 tsp salt
- 1 can chickpeas
- 1 cup tomatoes
- ½ cup feta cheese
- 1 zucchini
- 1 tablespoon basil

DIRECTIONS

1. In a bowl combine all ingredients together and mix well
2. Serve with dressing

Serves: **2**

Prep Time: **5**   Minutes

Cook Time: **5**   Minutes

Total Time: **10** Minutes

INGREDIENTS

- 1 cup cooked FARRO
- 1 bay leaf
- 1 shallot
- ¼ cup olive oil
- 2 cups arugula
- ¼ cup parmesan cheese
- ¼ cup basil
- ¼ cup parsley
- ¼ cup pecans

DIRECTIONS

1. **In a bowl combine all ingredients together and mix well**
2. **Serve with dressing**

Serves: **2**

Prep Time: **5** Minutes

Cook Time: **5** Minutes

Total Time: **10** Minutes

INGREDIENTS

- 1 head leaf lettuce
- 1 red bell pepper
- 2 mangoes
- ¼ green onion
- ¼ cup peanuts
- ¼ cup cilantro
- 1 cup peanut dressing

DIRECTIONS

1. In a bowl combine all ingredients together and mix well
2. Serve with dressing

SIMPLE PIZZA RECIPE

Serves: *6-8*

Prep Time: *10*   Minutes

Cook Time: *15*   Minutes

Total Time: *25*   Minutes

INGREDIENTS

- 1 pizza crust
- ½ cup tomato sauce
- ¼ black pepper
- 1 cup pepperoni slices
- 1 cup mozzarella cheese
- 1 cup olives

DIRECTIONS

1. Spread tomato sauce on the pizza crust
2. Place all the toppings on the pizza crust
3. Bake the pizza at 425 F for 12-15 minutes
4. When ready remove pizza from the oven and serve

ZUCCHINI PIZZA

Serves: **6-8**

Prep Time: **10**   Minutes

Cook Time: **15**   Minutes

Total Time: **25**   Minutes

INGREDIENTS

- 1 pizza crust
- ½ cup tomato sauce
- ¼ black pepper
- 1 cup zucchini slices
- 1 cup mozzarella cheese
- 1 cup olives

DIRECTIONS

1. Spread tomato sauce on the pizza crust
2. Place all the toppings on the pizza crust
3. Bake the pizza at 425 F for 12-15 minutes
4. When ready remove pizza from the oven and serve

Serves: *6-8*

Prep Time: *10*   Minutes

Cook Time: *15*   Minutes

Total Time: *25*   Minutes

INGREDIENTS

- 1 pizza crust
- ½ cup tomato sauce
- ¼ black pepper
- 1 cup cauliflower
- 1 cup mozzarella cheese
- 1 cup olives

DIRECTIONS

1. Spread tomato sauce on the pizza crust
2. Place all the toppings on the pizza crust
3. Bake the pizza at 425 F for 12-15 minutes
4. When ready remove pizza from the oven and serve

BROCCOLI RECIPE

Serves: **6-8**

Prep Time: **10**   Minutes

Cook Time: **15**   Minutes

Total Time: **25**   Minutes

INGREDIENTS

- 1 pizza crust
- ½ cup tomato sauce
- ¼ black pepper
- 1 cup broccoli
- 1 cup mozzarella cheese
- 1 cup olives

DIRECTIONS

1. Spread tomato sauce on the pizza crust
2. Place all the toppings on the pizza crust
3. Bake the pizza at 425 F for 12-15 minutes
4. When ready remove pizza from the oven and serve

TOMATOES & HAM PIZZA

Serves: *6-8*

Prep Time: *10*   Minutes

Cook Time: *15*   Minutes

Total Time: *25*   Minutes

INGREDIENTS

- 1 pizza crust
- ½ cup tomato sauce
- ¼ black pepper
- 1 cup pepperoni slices
- 1 cup tomatoes
- 6-8 ham slices
- 1 cup mozzarella cheese
- 1 cup olives

DIRECTIONS

1. Spread tomato sauce on the pizza crust
2. Place all the toppings on the pizza crust
3. Bake the pizza at 425 F for 12-15 minutes
4. When ready remove pizza from the oven and serve

LEEK SOUP

Serves: **4**

Prep Time: **10** Minutes

Cook Time: **20** Minutes

Total Time: **30** Minutes

INGREDIENTS

- 1 tablespoon olive oil
- 1 lb. leek
- ¼ red onion
- ½ cup all-purpose flour
- ¼ tsp salt
- ¼ tsp pepper
- 1 can vegetable broth
- 1 cup heavy cream

DIRECTIONS

1. In a saucepan heat olive oil and sauté onion until tender
2. Add remaining ingredients to the saucepan and bring to a boil
3. When all the vegetables are tender transfer to a blender and blend until smooth
4. Pour soup into bowls, garnish with parsley and serve

ZUCCHINI SOUP

Serves: **4**

Prep Time: **10** Minutes

Cook Time: **20** Minutes

Total Time: **30** Minutes

INGREDIENTS

- 1 tablespoon olive oil
- 1 lb. zucchini
- ¼ red onion
- ½ cup all-purpose flour
- ¼ tsp salt
- ¼ tsp pepper
- 1 can vegetable broth
- 1 cup heavy cream

DIRECTIONS

1. In a saucepan heat olive oil and sauté zucchini until tender
2. Add remaining ingredients to the saucepan and bring to a boil
3. When all the vegetables are tender transfer to a blender and blend until smooth
4. Pour soup into bowls, garnish with parsley and serve

RUTABAGA SOUP

Serves: **4**

Prep Time: **10**   Minutes

Cook Time: **20**   Minutes

Total Time: **30**   Minutes

INGREDIENTS

- 1 tablespoon olive oil
- 1 lb. rutabaga
- ¼ red onion
- ½ cup all-purpose flour
- ¼ tsp salt
- ¼ tsp pepper
- 1 can vegetable broth
- 1 cup heavy cream

DIRECTIONS

1. In a saucepan heat olive oil and sauté onion until tender
2. Add remaining ingredients to the saucepan and bring to a boil
3. When all the vegetables are tender transfer to a blender and blend until smooth
4. Pour soup into bowls, garnish with parsley and serve

Serves: **4**

Prep Time: **10**   Minutes

Cook Time: **20**   Minutes

Total Time: **30**   Minutes

INGREDIENTS

- 1 tablespoon olive oil
- 1 lb. carrots
- ¼ red onion
- ½ cup all-purpose flour
- ¼ tsp salt
- ¼ tsp pepper
- 1 can vegetable broth
- 1 cup heavy cream

DIRECTIONS

1. In a saucepan heat olive oil and sauté carrots until tender
2. Add remaining ingredients to the saucepan and bring to a boil
3. When all the vegetables are tender transfer to a blender and blend until smooth
4. Pour soup into bowls, garnish with parsley and serve

YAMS SOUP

Serves: **4**

Prep Time: **10** Minutes

Cook Time: **20** Minutes

Total Time: **30** Minutes

INGREDIENTS

- 1 tablespoon olive oil
- 1 lb. yams
- ¼ red onion
- ½ cup all-purpose flour
- ¼ tsp salt
- ¼ tsp pepper
- 1 can vegetable broth
- 1 cup heavy cream

DIRECTIONS

1. In a saucepan heat olive oil and sauté onion until tender
2. Add remaining ingredients to the saucepan and bring to a boil
3. When all the vegetables are tender transfer to a blender and blend until smooth
4. Pour soup into bowls, garnish with parsley and serve

SMOOTHIES

PEANUT BUTTER SMOOTHIE

Serves: **1**

Prep Time: **5** Minutes

Cook Time: **5** Minutes

Total Time: **10** Minutes

INGREDIENTS

- 1 tsp vanilla
- 1/3 cup milk
- 1/3 cup Greek yogurt
- 1 cup ice
- 2 tbs peanut butter
- 1 banana

DIRECTIONS

1. In a blender place all ingredients and blend until smooth
2. Pour smoothie in a glass and serve

PINEAPPLE SMOOTHIE

Serves: **1**

Prep Time: **5** Minutes

Cook Time: **5** Minutes

Total Time: **10** Minutes

INGREDIENTS

- 1/3 cup almond milk
- ½ cup carrots
- 2 tbs oats
- 1/3 cup yogurt
- ½ cup pineapple juice
- 1 banana
- 1 cup berries
- 1 ½ cup spinach leaves
- 1 cup strawberries
- 3 tbs flax seed
- 2 tbs chia seeds
- 1 cup ice

DIRECTIONS

1. In a blender place all ingredients and blend until smooth
2. Pour smoothie in a glass and serve

Serves: **1**

Prep Time: **5**   Minutes

Cook Time: **5**   Minutes

Total Time: **10**   Minutes

INGREDIENTS

- 1 ½ cups orange juice
- ½ cup yogurt
- 1 tbs sugar
- 1 banana
- 1 ½ cups berries

DIRECTIONS

1. In a blender place all ingredients and blend until smooth
2. Pour smoothie in a glass and serve

STRAWBERRY SMOOTHIE

Serves: **1**

Prep Time: **5** Minutes

Cook Time: **5** Minutes

Total Time: **10** Minutes

INGREDIENTS

- 1 cup yogurt
- 1/3 cup skim milk
- 1 banana
- ½ cup strawberries

DIRECTIONS

1. In a blender place all ingredients and blend until smooth
2. Pour smoothie in a glass and serve

MANGO SMOOTHIE

Serves: **1**

Prep Time: **5** Minutes

Cook Time: **5** Minutes

Total Time: **10** Minutes

INGREDIENTS

- 1 cup coconut water
- 5 tbs orange juice
- 1 cup ice
- 1 cup Greek yogurt
- 1 cup mango

DIRECTIONS

1. In a blender place all ingredients and blend until smooth
2. Pour smoothie in a glass and serve

SPINACH SMOOTHIE

Serves: *1*

Prep Time: *5*   Minutes

Cook Time: *5*   Minutes

Total Time: *10* Minutes

INGREDIENTS

- 1/3 cup milk
- 1/3 cup Greek yogurt
- 2 tbs butter
- 1 banana
- 1/3 cup strawberries
- 1/3 cup spinach

DIRECTIONS

1. In a blender place all ingredients and blend until smooth
2. Pour smoothie in a glass and serve

OATS SMOOTHIE

Serves: *1*

Prep Time: *5*   Minutes

Cook Time: *5*   Minutes

Total Time: *10*   Minutes

INGREDIENTS

- 1 banana
- 10 strawberries
- ½ cup oats
- 1 ½ tbs flaxseed
- 1 cup skim milk
- 1 tsp vanilla
- 2 tsp honey

DIRECTIONS

1. In a blender place all ingredients and blend until smooth
2. Pour smoothie in a glass and serve

BERRY BEAN SMOOTHIE

Serves: *1*

Prep Time: **5**   Minutes

Cook Time: **5**   Minutes

Total Time: **10**   Minutes

INGREDIENTS

- 2 cup orange juice
- 2 tsp cinnamon
- 2 cups strawberries
- 4 tbs honey
- ¼ tsp nutmeg
- 1 cup ice
- 15 oz beans

DIRECTIONS

1. **In a blender place all ingredients and blend until smooth**
2. **Pour smoothie in a glass and serve**

ORANGE SMOOTHIE

Serves: **1**

Prep Time: **5** Minutes

Cook Time: **5** Minutes

Total Time: **10** Minutes

INGREDIENTS

- 2 oranges
- 1 cup ice
- 3 tsp vanilla
- 1 banana
- ½ cup milk

DIRECTIONS

1. In a blender place all ingredients and blend until smooth
2. Pour smoothie in a glass and serve

Serves: **1**

Prep Time: **5** Minutes

Cook Time: **5** Minutes

Total Time: **10** Minutes

INGREDIENTS

- 1 cup ice
- 3 tbs avocado
- 2 tbs chia seeds
- 1/3 cup milk
- ½ cup cauliflower
- 1 cup blueberries

DIRECTIONS

1. In a blender place all ingredients and blend until smooth
2. Pour smoothie in a glass and serve

THANK YOU FOR READING THIS BOOK!